PICTURES ·FROM ·THE ·PAST

Rural Li

PICTURES · FROM · THE · PAST

Rural Life

John Seymour

SELECT
EDITIONS

First published in Great Britain in 1991
by Collins & Brown Limited

ISBN 1 85648 127 1

The pictures in this book are archive photographs and, to preserve the character and
quality of the original, have not been re-touched in any way.

Acknowledgements
The author and publishers are grateful to Bob Copper for permission to reproduce
copyright extracts from his book *A Song for Every Season* (Heinemann 1971).

All photographs were supplied by the Hulton Picture Company and are available as
framed prints. For more information and to place your orders contact:

Framed Prints
Hulton Picture Company
Unique House
21-31 Woodfield Road
London W9 2BA

Tel: 071 266 2660
Fax: 071 266 2414

This edition published 1993 by
The Promotional Reprint Co Ltd,
exclusively for Selecta Book Ltd,
Folly Road,Roundway, Devizes,
Wiltshire, SN10 2HR

Reprint 1995

Printed in Hong Kong

CONTENTS

INTRODUCTION

When I look at the earliest of the photographs in this book – at those, for example, taken in the mid-nineteenth century – I have the feeling that I am looking into a time capsule. When I look at the pictures from the 1920s, 30s and 40s, on the other hand, I feel – but that's *now*! But of course it is not now, for those same pictures seem like museum pieces to the young people of today.

I think that it was round about the end of the Second World War that the break occurred: when farmers, and indeed farm workers, began to dress and carry themselves in such a way that they could not be distinguished from townspeople. Before that war they certainly could.

LEFT: *'The ploughman homeward plods his weary way.' Only the horses do the plodding. Before the men can go home to their tea they will have to water the horses, take them into the stable and unharness them, bait them with a mixture of crushed oats and chaff and plenty of hay, rub them down well with straw whisps and clean the harness.*

FAR LEFT: *The shadows are short as the last load of the morning is carried from hayfield to stackyard. A trace horse has been hitched on in front of the shafter as no doubt there was a hill, or some soft ground, to negotiate.*

For one thing they were a lot poorer. Farm workers before the Second World War were paid a miserly thirty shillings a week (a town labourer got £5 – a hundred shillings). True, they all had good gardens: they could hardly have survived without them. They grew their own potatoes, onions, runner beans and winter greens, and many of them still kept poultry. Some of the older farm workers in 1930 still kept a pig, and what a boon that was to a hard-pressed family with many mouths to feed. The great fat hams and long sides of bacon hung up in the cottage kitchens were an insurance against real hunger. The farm worker, if he became unemployed, did not get the dole like the city worker did. And he would quite likely be put out of his tied cottage.

Even the farmer – particularly the tenant farmer, and most farmers were tenants – was not so very much better-off. Many of them, during the Great Depression, were only saved from bankruptcy by the fact that it was not worth bankrupting them. They might have managed to keep an old banger of a Ford car on the road, and have had an annual day in London, probably going to the Smithfield Show to look at fat cattle, but that was about the limit of their high living. Certainly no trips to the Costa Brava.

And yet when I talk to old country people today, so many of them say: 'We had more fun in those days!' Certainly that's the way I remember it. The happiest days of my life were when I was living in English farm workers' cottages and doing the same work as they did. They were the nicest people I have ever known. To be accepted by them as a workmate and a friend was a great honour and privilege. I would not have swapped my lot with any city person.

'Let the wealthy and great
Roll in splendour and state;
I envy them not I declare it!'

Were they 'good old days' or 'bad old days'? Well, they were a bit of both. It was wrong that men should have to do hard – and often very

ABOVE: *This summer idyll was obviously posed. It was taken in 1857 for* Grundy's English Views.

skilled – labour twelve hours a day for a pittance of a wage. It was hard that women had to scrimp and scheme to get the shoes on their children's feet or to feed the family properly. It was wrong, too, that the farmers who employed the men should be forced to pay them miserable wages because they could hardly make ends meet themselves. The one thing they *had* to find was the rent, which had to go to the land-owners whatever happened. The latter were the only ones who never went short: they rode high on the hog!

I think it was the women I admired most. Even as late as 1930, they swarmed over the harvest fields after the binder and gleaned the fallen corn; whenever there was fruit to pick they went fruit-picking. They had to get their husbands off to work by six o'clock in the morning (horsemen had to be at work by 5.30 – to groom and bait their animals!), get their kids off to school, do the housework, and have a hot meal ready for hungry man and children at night. They had to mend and make clothes: most of the children, and indeed the adults too, had to make do with cast-off clothing from better-off people. The village jumble sale was of real importance. And yet they managed to look good, and comport themselves with dignity and self-possession.

The farm men, too, used to take their poverty as a challenge. The best of them poached: pheasants, partridges, hares – anything that would bring in some money – and rabbits for their own table. They craved to work overtime: if a man could knock up two pounds a week over harvest by working fifteen hours a day he was delighted. They spent what little spare time they had working in their own gardens.

Many townspeople believe that because farming is mechanized today it is therefore

LEFT: *Before piped water, people drew their water from the stream. The people here, at Shoreham in Sussex, seem to have time to stand and stare.*

ABOVE: *The carter fills his water cart in 1905, while his horse cools his feet. The butt, or big barrel, on the left is being soaked to prevent it shrinking and falling apart.*

more skilled than it used to be. Nothing could be further from the truth. The modern ploughman spends day after day sitting enclosed in a cab with earphones clapped over his ears, driving up and down, endlessly up and down. Anyone could do it. To plough with a pair of horses – particularly with a balance plough that had no wheels – was highly skilled work. To lay a hedge, quickly and well, to build a stone wall, to build and thatch a hay stack or a corn rick, to shear sheep with hand shears and do enough in a day to earn a living and not nick them: these and a hundred other tasks were skilled jobs if ever there were such.

So where was the 'good old days' side of it? Well, the work itself was very rewarding. People took immense pride in it. And the comradeship was something that is hard to describe: it was a real thing and something that I can never forget. You would go far to find the like of it today. And the fact that each man saw the beginning and

LEFT: *Making raised hotbeds for forcing vegetables at Stable Farm, Thatcham (Berkshire) in 1908. The system, widely practised in France, never really caught on in England.*

RIGHT: *In 1909, when this photograph of turkey pluckers was taken, there was evidently no great labour shortage.*

BELOW: *Most of these hard-looking characters are members of an itinerant threshing gang.*

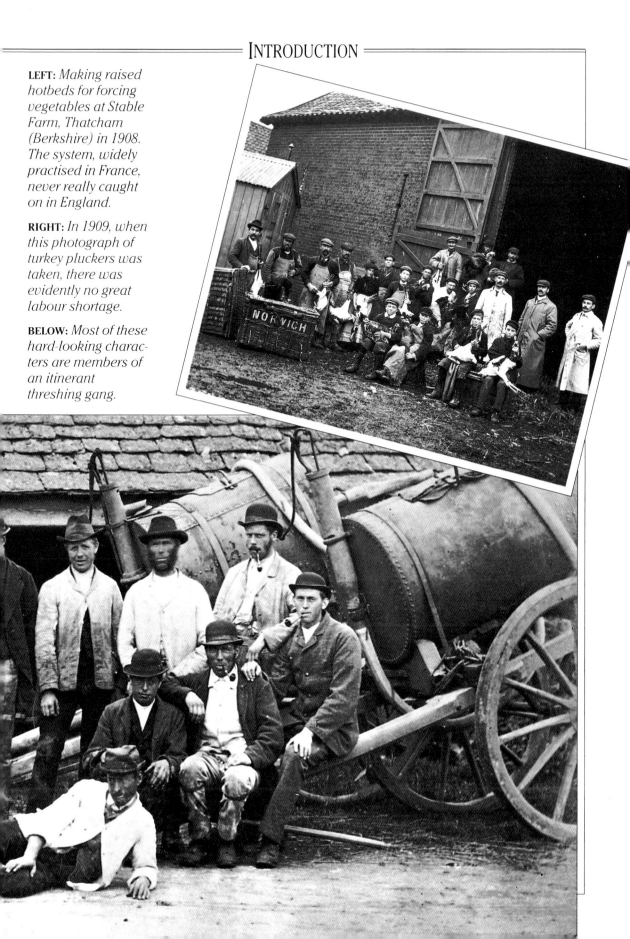

the end of every job he undertook made the work far more satisfying, and at least the farm labourer lived in the knowledge that he earned his bread in the sweat of his brow, unlike so many other people.

So much has changed in the last sixty years that it is hard to believe that many of the scenes portrayed in this book took place within living memory. The photographs have been chosen specifically to recapture the period: the hard grind of farming life, the skills and traditions that have now all but disappeared from our countryside and, above all, the spirit of a close-knit rural community.

'Good luck unto the ploughboys wherever they
    may be,
They will take a winsome lass for to sit upon
    their knee,
And with a jug of beer, boys, they'll whistle and
    they'll sing,
For the ploughboy is as happy as a prince or a
    king!'

LEFT: *Hard tiled floors, simple rustic furniture, open fire, and beer or cider drawn straight from the barrel: this was comfort enough for working country people. In my boyhood, singing was the only entertainment in most pubs.*

ABOVE: *A rural congregation could sing 'Now all is safely gathered in' with a good conscience. The harvest festival really meant something to men and women who had toiled with horses and pitchforks 16 hours a day for a month.*

WORKING THE LAND

Unlike most of Europe, England was a land of huge estates and big tenanted farms worked by landless labourers. The latter were by far the lowest paid people in the country and the hardest worked. But the farm worker probably had a free cottage (which he could be kicked out of by a whim of his employer), he could keep a pig and some poultry in his garden, and he always grew good vegetables. He worked in the open air, in beautiful countryside, and if he was a man of spirit he could poach a rabbit or a pheasant when he wanted one.

I was brought up among such people, and in a long life I have never encountered finer men and women. Poor they may have been, materially, but they were rich in the things that mattered: true skill, intense pride in their craft, complete honesty and great self-respect. To be accepted as an equal and a comrade by them was, to me, a privilege far greater than to have consorted with kings.

RIGHT: *As cities grew in the nineteenth century, so vegetables began to be produced on a large scale. These baskets would be bound for the nearest railway station to be shipped off to some big city.*

RIGHT: *Free-range at its very best! Hens peck for food outside this farm in Snowdonia.*

ABOVE: *Threshed straw is being raised up to a stack, from where it is carried to the cattle yards, pig styes or stables. Wheat straw was used as bedding; oats or barley straw was fed to the animals. Nowadays most straw is burnt.*

LEFT AND BELOW: *Both these photographs were originally published in* Grundy's English Views *in 1857.*

RIGHT: *Incredibly, this photograph was taken in 1938, some fifty years after the photographs on the opposite page, yet from the style of dress all these farm workers could have been contemporaries. My memory goes back to the end of the first World War, and I never saw a farm worker in a smock.*

LEFT: *True Romany people, living in the ornate and heavy Reading vans. Such people still had traces of their ancient language.*

BELOW: *Until the late 1800s, gypsies lived in 'bender tents' made by sticking sticks in the ground and bending them over.*

BELOW: *By 1901, when this photograph was taken, the* vardo, *or wagon – in this case, a barrel top – has arrived, although a bender tent can still be seen.*

Hop-picking

Many people think that beer is made from hops. It is not. It is brewed from malted (sprouted) barley and flavoured with hops.

Hops are now grown chiefly in Kent, where the following photographs were taken, and in Herefordshire. The crop used to require a huge labour force for the picking season, and this was supplied in Kent by people from the East End of London – a paid country holiday for thousands who would otherwise never have left the city streets. And it *was* a holiday: after the day's work there was singing and fun in the village pub and old people still remember it with delight. Whole families would return to the same farm year after year.

RIGHT: *After picking, the hop flowers were dried in oast houses like the one at the back of this photograph. These beautiful structures have now been replaced by electric or oil-fired drying machines.*

LEFT: *The hop-pickers – mostly women and children – stripped off the bitter flowers into canvas troughs. Nowadays the vines are cut down to the ground and carted off to the barn, where the flowers are stripped off by machine.*

RIGHT: *Men used to work on stilts to fix the intricate web of twine for the hop vines to grow up. Now they are more likely to work from the fore-end loader of a tractor.*

BELOW: *The 'gyrotiller', two examples of which are shown here, came in towards the end of the nineteenth century. The tines went down into the subsoil and churned it up, breaking* up any plough pan. I can remember seeing one working in Suffolk after the Second World War but now, I imagine, it is as extinct as the dinosaurus.

RIGHT: *The tractor, now an integral part of any farming landscape, did not become common until after the First World War.*

ABOVE: *Watercress farms, such as this early one, sprang up in the valleys of Hampshire and Sussex, where the clear chalk streams could be made to spread out and flood the shallow beds.*

RIGHT: *Cider-making was a most important activity in Kent, the West Country, and the Welsh borders. Nowadays most cider apples are grown on contract for the big factories, but plenty of good 'scrumpy', or strong unsweetened cider, is still made on the farms.*

ABOVE: *Cherries being picked in a Kentish orchard. Kent, often called 'the Garden of England', was once rich in fruit trees.*

RIGHT: *It was the steam-tackle that began the demise of the horse as a working farm animal. The massive traction engine did not actually have to go on the soil: the multiple plough, which could plough ten furrows at a time, was dragged across the field by a wire rope attached to a moveable pulley.*

ABOVE: *The British spud. This is in Essex in 1936. The potatoes were ploughed, or more likely spun, out with a horse-drawn potato lifter, picked up into baskets and carried to the clamp against which the lifters are leaning to eat their well-earned lunch. Farm workers welcomed the potato harvest as a means of adding to a small income before the winter set in. In 1936 an Essex farm worker was paid thirty shillings (£1.50) a week. Even in those days it was a miserable wage.*

The haysel, or hay harvest, preceded the corn harvest and, in the damp English climate, could be an anxious time. Judgement, hard labour and luck were all needed to prevent the hay from spoiling or going mouldy.

RIGHT: *Before the days of horse-drawn or machine-powered mower, the thick high grass had to be cut by scythe – a tough job for anyone. This photograph was taken in Westmoreland around the turn of the century.*

ABOVE: *Hay being loaded to be taken to the stackyard. A sled is being used – a primitive vehicle, but much used on small farms in very hilly country. This photograph was taken near Ambleside in the Lake District before the First World War.*

RIGHT: *After drying in the fields, the hay was carried to the stackyard where it was carefully built up into beautifully shaped stacks, either round or oblong, and then thatched with straw. Such stacks could last for years, although the hay was normally all used by the spring of the next year. Here a loaded wagon returns from the stackyard while a full one waits to go to the field.*

ABOVE: *Unloading hay into the loft above either stable or cattle shed. Later it would be fed down to the animals below. Carts such as this would once be found on every farm in England: farming would have been well nigh impossible without them. They were most commonly used for tipping out 'muck' (manure).*

THE COUNTRYSIDE AT PLAY

B efore the days of television and video, before even the crystal set (I remember hearing the first one when I was nine), country people did not require anything very elaborate to amuse themselves. The garden party on the vicarage lawn, the amateur concert in the village hall, the annual fête with nothing more exciting than bowling for a pig, and the occasional visit of a travelling fair was all people expected in the way of excitement. I have fond memories of concerts at which the village Caruso gave us his rendering of 'Come into the garden, Maud!', followed by 'I am the captain of my soul'; and many's the time I heard how the Boy stood on the Burning Deck, and the sad tale of the Wreck of the Hesperous. That was culture enough for most of us.

RIGHT: *Simple sports caused great hilarity. But it was all good fun.*

LEFT: *The sweet stall at the vicar's garden party rakes in the money – all in a good cause.*

RIGHT: *Before any social event, the kitchens of the village would be a hive of activity as the women prepared mounds of sandwiches and cakes. If the fête involved competitions for the best baking, rivalry could be intense: it was a brave man or woman who would agree to act as judge.*

BELOW: *A whole ox being roasted at the Stratford-on-Avon 'Mop Fair', or Hiring Fair, in 1913. Farm workers, tradesmen and domestic servants, wearing some emblem of their trade, came to fairs such as this to meet would-be employers. Away from the main business of the day, roundabouts and side-shows provided a rare treat for the large crowds who came simply to enjoy the fun.*

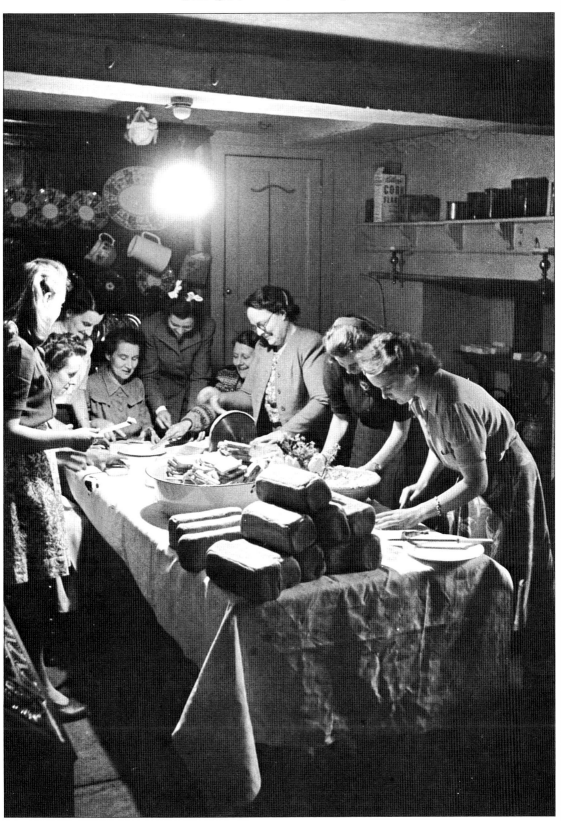

The Village Inn

'Come all you honest labouring men that work
    hard all the day,
And join me at the Barley Mow to pass an hour
    away . . .'

(From *A Song for Every Season*)

The traditional British tavern was a place of
pure magic: good, well-mannered, witty talk of
crops, or land, or poaching pheasants; the
delicious smell of wood or coal fire, good beer
and shag tobacco: all this added up for me to
the essence of true civilization.

ABOVE: *The game of darts is a recent
innovation. Card games, often played for a
few pennies (and a few pennies were all the
players had) were common. Many country ale
houses (beer and cider licence only) had the
atmosphere of a family gathering rather than
a public place; and it was rare that one
encountered strangers.*

LEFT: *With no ready-made entertainment, country folk had to invent their own. Skittles, dominoes and other games were as much a part of the pub's attraction as the beer.*

ABOVE: *The man on the right is wearing what were variously called leggins, buskins or, in East Anglia, 'Elijahs'. Beer glasses were unusual in country pubs: earthenware – or, in some places, pewter – mugs, now collectors' items, were far more common. Regular customers often had their own mugs, specially reserved for them.*

Family A. NEWICK

LEFT: *The village band, its instruments no doubt lovingly polished and its uniforms specially washed and ironed for the occasion, marches proudly at the head of a procession through Hinton St George in Somerset. This was to celebrate the Coronation in 1953 – although almost any excuse would do!*

Village and town bands are still an important feature of life in many areas of Britain, particularly in the North of England, and can be credited with instilling a lifelong love of music in countless thousands of amateurs over the years.

ABOVE: *In 1908, when these Gloucestershire morris dancers were photographed, the traditional folk arts of Britain were at their lowest ebb: the new city folk felt such things were beneath them. Since then there has been a nationwide revival of interest in traditional music and dance, and morris men (and women – a real break with tradition) flourish up and down the land.*

May Day

May Day – the coming of spring – has been celebrated since time immemorial; indeed, many of the customs associated with it, such as maypole dancing, the hobby horse and various fertility rites, are pre-Christian in origin. There was no doubt a magical element in such celebrations as these. With the discovery of agriculture women and men began to practice sympathetic magic to secure the germination and good growth of crops. These and other traditions were sternly suppressed by the Puritans in the seventeenth century, although a few attempts have been made to revive them in the last century.

BELOW: *The maypole being carried to the village green at Elston, Bedfordshire, on May Day 1934. The Puritan writer John Bunyan, who came from there, would have been horrified at such proceedings.*

LEFT: *Ready for the May Day parade at Mattock, near Bath, in 1907. The splendour of the great horses was part of the occasion.*

ABOVE: *The carrying of the hobby horse from door to door somehow managed to survive Puritanism in a very few places.*

LEFT: *When I was a boy you could be almost sure of skating on local ponds or dykes in East Anglia every winter. Mr Harry Gooch's ice yacht, seen here sailing on one of the 'washes' (flooded fields) near Spalding in Lincolnshire in 1908, would not be of much use today.*

ABOVE: *The 'Fenland skaters' that I used to hear about in my childhood have hung up their skates to rust long since. Only about twice since the Second World War has the ice been strong enough to bear, yet before 1940 great long-distance races were held along the Fenland waterways nearly every year.*

LEFT: *The beaters (known as 'brushers' in East Anglia) at a farmers' shoot in Norfolk in 1943. It was their job to advance in a line through the woods and other coverts, beating the trees with their sticks and making a noise so as to drive the pheasants over the line of guns.*

ABOVE: *There is something ritualistic and rather pagan about this sort of hunting, as witness the extraordinary get-up of Mr and Mrs Fife and daughter at Nunnington Hall, Yorkshire, in 1923. But the countryman, posh or plebeian, has always had a liking for hunting animals.*

ABOVE: The beaters bring up refreshments at a 1926 shooting party. Penalties for poaching were severe: in the last century people were transported to Australia for poaching a pheasant.

RIGHT: The Devon and Somerset Hounds moving off in 1926. The scene would look much the same today: some things just never change. (Fox-hunting was once memorably described by Oscar Wilde as 'the unspeakable in full pursuit of the uneatable'.)

ABOVE: Mr J.G. Murray waits for the birds to be driven over him, while his loader stands by to replace the empty gun with a loaded one.

LEFT: *The beaters lug in the bag after a shoot in 1923. Hares are 'game' and you must have a game licence to shoot one. The legal definition includes mainly those creatures prized by the nobility: hare, roebuck and pheasant are classed as game; rabbit and woodpigeon are not. Hares must be hung for a week before cooking; rabbits must be eaten quickly, which indicates their humble status.*

RIGHT: *Whatever the quarry, hunting could be thirsty work.*

ABOVE: *Rabbiting. The sack carried by the man in the middle probably contained ferrets to drive the rabbits from their burrows.*

THE VILLAGE CRAFTSMAN

U ntil the First World War most villages were substantially self-sufficient. I can remember one Suffolk village that, even in my day, had a blacksmith, a corn miller, a maltster, carpenter-cum-undertaker, builder, thatcher, butcher who killed his own meat, boot-maker, hurdle-maker, tailor, baker, and carrier who went into Ipswich with a horse and van to do errands for people. Now not one of those trades survives in that particular village: the inhabitants have to go outside the village for everything they need.

Other craftsmen, such as a saddler and harness-maker, and a wheelwright and wagon-builder, might serve several villages. In some areas harness-makers would travel round to farms and spend several days every year mending all the harness – for without good harness, there could be no good farming.

RIGHT: *The village blacksmith was absolutely indispensable: the community could not have endured without him. Horses could not work unless he shod them, and in frosty weather he had to roughen their shoes to stop them slipping on the roads. He could also make or mend practically any implement the farmer needed. The forge itself was a kind of club for the locals: while waiting for their horses to be shod, people could gossip and exchange news.*

LEFT: *It is hard to find a harness-maker and saddler like this today. The working farm horse has almost disappeared, and all the beautiful old harness has been hung up on pub walls as ornament.*

ABOVE: *Hand-made working boots were expected to last two years of hard farm work. A new pair traditionally cost a farm worker two weeks' wages; not surprisingly, they were well cared for and would be patched up and repaired many times before they finally gave out.*

LEFT: *Grinding corn was a very time-consuming and boring occupation, so when wind and water were harnessed corn milling was one of the first things they were applied to. Milling requires great skill, and (even if he was accused of returning short measure occasionally) the miller was a respected man.*

BELOW: *Great skill was needed to 'dress' the stones: the top stone, or 'runner', being hove over on its back and its grooves, and those of the bed stone, carefully chipped out with a small steel pick.*

RIGHT: *This mill, like all such structures, did its work quietly, causing no pollution, and without the use of fossil fuel.*

Thatching

Nothing keeps a house so warm and snug, or looks so attractive and quintessentially 'English', as a thick coat of thatch. Once the cheapest form of roofing material, however, thatch is now a luxury; and the skills of the thatcher, previously seen in many areas, are increasingly disappearing from our countryside.

Norfolk reed (*Phragmites communis*) is the best of all thatching material, and far better than wheat or rye straw. A roof of it will last seventy years or more. It is still cut in the Norfolk Broads country, but much of the straw used for thatching in Britain today is imported from Holland.

LEFT: *Reed cutters come home from the marshes. This photograph, and the one below, were taken by the Victorian naturalist, Dr Peter Henry Emerson.*

BELOW: *Stacking Norfolk reed.*

RIGHT: *Hazel spars, or brortches, are driven into the thatch to hold the ridging in place.*

Charcoal is made by burning wood and keeping it, while burning, short of air. It was – and still is – lonely work: charcoal burners live rough, cooking and caring for themselves and sleeping when the fires give them a chance, for as soon as one huge pile of wooden stakes is burned through there is another to light.

RIGHT: *The huge pile of wooden stakes is covered with hay (or 'litter'). This is then covered with clay to keep out the air.*

ABOVE: *Damping down a fire to keep it burning steadily and evenly – the secret of successful charcoal-burning. When these photographs were taken in 1951, charcoal was still being made in the open. Now the few people who do make charcoal burn it in huge iron drums.*

The countryman traditionally had the right to collect such firewood as he could get 'by hook or by crook' – i.e. he was allowed to hook down dead branches but not to fell trees.

RIGHT: *This photograph was taken in 1939, when war was imminent and it was all hands to the woods if people wanted to keep warm.*

BELOW: *Forest workers break off to brew up some tea. The chainsaw has made much of the woodsman's skill redundant.*

ABOVE: *The sweet chestnut grows quickly, cleaves easily and lasts long. Hurdle-maker Bill Slingsby, photographed in 1950, is seen here removing the bark from poles by pushing them through a device known as a hopple-shave. The poles would then be split down the grain and fitted into hurdles by means of morticing and a few nails. The hurdles, sold mainly to sheep farmers for enclosing sheep in turnip fields, would last for years.*

ANIMALS

The immense strength of the huge and magnificent heavy horses of these islands – the descendants of the Great Horse of the armoured knight – made it easy for them to do most of the jobs asked of them. The Shire, the Clydesdale, the Suffolk Punch were, and still are, the finest draught horses in the world. Alas, the oil-guzzling tractor has made them all but extinct as working animals.

As for animals that provide us with meat, milk, wool and leather, there are more recognized distinctive breeds of sheep in the British Isles than in the whole of the rest of the world put together. British beef breeds of cattle, descended from oxen specially bred for pulling the plough, have imprinted their genes in most countries of the world, although they have been in retreat during the last seventy years before the all-conquering black-and-white Friesian. Pigs and poultry were kept, when most of these photographs were taken, in conditions very close to the ones Nature had intended them for. This is no longer the case and too many farm animals are now subjected to acute sensory deprivation.

RIGHT: *Neither of these men carry whips. They do not need them – I never saw an English working horseman with a whip. A quiet 'gid up, ol' gal!' to make her go, or 'cupwhee!', meaning come to the left, or 'waardee!' (go to the right) was all that was required.*

'That man would be a shepherd must have a
    valiant heart,
He must not be faint-hearted but boldly play
    his part!
He must not be faint-hearted, be it rain or frost
    or snow,
There's no ale on the wolds where the stormy
    winds do blow.'

Gloucestershire song

LEFT AND ABOVE: *The mountain farmer is utterly dependent on his dogs, for without them he would have no hope of mustering what are really no more than wild animals from miles of broken country.*

LEFT: *Sheep, which can graze on the roughest of mountain pasture, are a wonderful source of wool, meat and milk (for those nations that still have enough sense to milk them). But the life of the sheep farmer is far from being an easy one: up at the crack of dawn, out in all weathers and often far from home. It requires stamina – and a well-trained dog – to drive the sheep of the Welsh mountains down the valley for washing and shearing.*

ABOVE: *The sheep fair at Findon, in Sussex, was the biggest in the South of England, and the year this photograph was taken (1935) 10,000 sheep were sold there. In the North there were, and still are, much larger fairs, at which huge numbers of sheep are sold to the farmers of the South for breeding or for fattening on their better land.*

LEFT AND RIGHT: *These photographs were taken by the Walmsley brothers of Ambleside around the turn of the century. To shear sheep cleanly without nicking them, with either these hand shear or the modern power clipper, is taxing work for even the strongest man.*

BELOW: *The arduous job of shearing is eased if the sheep have been washed in a stream a week or two before they are sheared. The wool is better, too.*

Markets

The auction mart is a fairly recent invention. Within recent living memory towns and villages had stock fairs, held in the wide market street, to which animals were driven from the surrounding countryside. Bargaining might go on for hours, but when the deal was finally agreed the bargain was 'struck' by the two men concerned striking the palms of their right hands together. In the West and North, 'luck' money was always expected by the buyer: a pound or two was handed over by the vendor and the two of them would probably spend this in the nearest pub.

Nowadays the auction mart has taken over: the animals are driven into a ring and sold by auction by a professional auctioneer, or else sold pen by pen as the auctioneer and the prospective buyers (and assorted hangers-on) move along.

RIGHT: *Bampton Horse Fair, Devon, in 1925. Exmoor ponies, which have lived wild on the Moor all their lives, have been rounded up, broken to the bridle, and led in here for sale.*

BOTTOM RIGHT: *Store cattle (i.e. cattle not yet fattened) driven in for sale in Bampton in 1922. These cattle, having been walked in gently from the surrounding countryside, look far more serene and contented than the modern bullock who is jammed into a crowded cattle truck, jolted maybe a hundred miles, debouched in a pen and then driven into the ring with an electric prod. But 'time is money' nowadays and why should anyone consider the animal's feelings?*

BELOW: *Hill sheep, probably of the Lonk breed, in the auction ring at Clitheroe in 1955.*

LEFT: *An idyllic scene of rural England. Nowadays, with intensive farming, scenes like this are increasingly rare: you are more likely to see huge herds of cattle in a vast field reminiscent of an American prairie.*

ABOVE: *Cow, horse and hens jostle comfortably together in this farmyard scene from* Grundy's English Views *of 1857. Nowadays farmyards seem to be far more neat and regimented – but they are also far less atmospheric.*

BELOW: *How milkmaids never dressed! These ladies are got up specially for the occasion at the Dairy Show at Agricultural Hall, Norwich, in 1912.*

RIGHT: *This is closer to how milkmaids dressed – although she really should have been wearing a cap. It was a good woman or man who could hand-milk a dozen cows twice a day. Now a person might milk 100 animals by machine, but it is tedious work and there is no pleasure in it.*

BELOW: *The milk churns go off to the station at Uttoxeter early one morning in 1925. Milkers never got a lie-in and each year had 365 working days in it (excepting leap years).*

Agricultural shows

Agricultural shows, small-scale and large-scale, were – and still are – a chance for farmers to show off their best livestock. Animals, specially groomed for the big day, are paraded around the ring to the critical gaze of experts (who include friends and neighbours as well as the official judge); and the coveted rosettes denoting prize-winners are highly sought after.

The shows often include tests of skill as well as pedigree – sheepdog trials, ploughing matches, gymkhana events, show-jumping, flower arranging and baking contests and many more. Something for all the family!

RIGHT: *'A full belly makes a strong back!' These magificent beasts are having a feed of hay before taking part in a ploughing match.*

BELOW: *The Champion Beast of the 1924 Norwich Fat Cattle Show is proudly posed for the camera.*

LEFT: *Another champion is recorded for posterity.*

RIGHT: *The partnership between Man and Horse has endured for thousands of years to the benefit of both. This photograph shows improvised 'showshoes', made out of an old sack, being fitted to the patient horse of a timber-hauling team.*

'Come all ye honest ploughmen – old
   England's fate ye hold!
Who labour in the winter time in stormy
   winds and cold,
To clothe our fields with plenty – our
   farmyards to renew,
That bread may not be wanting, behold the
   Painful Plough.'
                    From A Song for Every Season

ABOVE: *Painful it may have been, but I knew an old ploughman in Essex, over eighty and retired, who used to cry when he heard a team of horses clattering by his cottage window, he so wanted to go with them. There is no joy like ploughing a straight, clean furrow behind two noble horses and laying over the bright shiny soil. This photograph was taken in the 1890s, probably in the Welsh Marches.*

RIGHT: *The light land area of south-west Norfolk was always a great place for turkeys. In times of old, thousands of them were walked to London to be sold. It is said that they picked up weight during the journey.*

ABOVE: *Geese are devils to pluck, as the boy on the right seems to be finding out. This photograph was taken in 1911, long before the invention of the plucking machine.*

Bee-keeping

Long before Man domesticated bees, people collected wild honey – they still do where wild bees have survived. Wild bees occupy holes in trees or under rocks, but people in tropical countries still hang up hollowed-out logs for them to nest in: this, no doubt, was the beginning of bee-keeping. Although we might not think it when we get well stung, the honey bee is among Man's best friends. Not only does she provide us with that delicious thing, honey – and also the best wax in the world – but she also pollinates our crops and fruit trees. And there is nothing to beat the honey you take from the hives in your own cottage garden!

RIGHT: *The Langstroth hive enables the colony to be inspected and also makes it possible to extract the honey without killing the brood and without destroying the wax comb.*

BELOW: *The straw bee-hive was cheap – anybody could make one – and it was warm for the bees. However, it is now discouraged because the bees cannot be inspected for the disease of foul brood. The conical straw 'hats' are to keep the rain off.*

HARVEST HOME

*'And in the time of Harvest how cheerfully we
	go,
Some with hooks and some with crooks and
	some with scythes to mow,
And when our corn is free from harm, we have
	not far to roam,
We'll all away to celebrate the welcome
	Harvest Home!'*
From A Song for Every Season

Before the coming of the combine harvester, the corn harvest was a worrying affair. Corn (in England the word means wheat, barley, oats and rye – not maize, as it does in America) cannot be cut or otherwise handled when it is wet and, in a wet August, this could mean that the grain could go rotten, or even start to germinate in the ear, before it could be harvested. The corn harvest was a time of intense hard work; and the joy, among both farmers and farm workers, when the corn was safely in the stack or barn, was great.

RIGHT: *A good corn rick was a work of art, and if you botched it the leaning or sagging structure might be there for months to rebuke you. Farm workers would spend their Sunday afternoons walking round the parish admiring or criticising each other's productions and the man whose rick needed to be shored up with poles to keep it from falling over would never live it down. The walls must lean outwards to avoid the rain, the outer wall of sheaves must slope down towards the outside for the same reason, the corners, if a rectangular stack, must be sharp and straight, the roof perfectly pitched and thatched. To the farmer a stackyard full of bountiful corn stacks was the most beautiful sight in the world.*

LEFT: *A good man with a scythe could mow an acre of corn a day, which was twice as much as he could have done with the more primitive sickle. But twenty or more mowers might sweep through the cornfields in a long line, led by the oldest one – the Lord of the Harvest. The scythe had to be sharpened frequently on a wetstone, but the job was welcomed as a respite from back-breaking labour.*

RIGHT: *This old man, in 1929, is bundling the straw ready for thatching. Straw that was to be used for thatching – either for the stacks or for buildings – was threshed without being put right through the threshing machine, so that the straw would not be broken.*

BELOW: *The sheaves had to be stooked – that is, stood up in short double-rows so that the ears and straw could dry out in the sun and wind. Wheat and barley could be carted and stacked almost immediately, but oats had to 'churched three times in the stook' – in other words, to stand for three Sundays.*

LEFT: *The corn was generally loaded by the older, more experienced men. The younger men pitched, flinging up the sheaves from the stooks.*

ABOVE: *When tractors became common after the First World War, one of the first jobs they were put to was pulling a binder.*

ABOVE: *The man in front of the threshing drum is working a small grinding mill. Normally the grain was stored in the barn until required.*

RIGHT: *Until the coming of the combine harvester, country women exercized the age-old right of gleaning – picking up grain that had been missed after the corn had been carted. They either took the grain to the mill to be ground or threw it to their chickens. A farmer who horse-raked the field or ploughed the stubble in the first fortnight after harvest was considered very mean. This picture was taken in the 1850s; I saw gleaners in Essex as late as 1930.*

ABOVE: *Picking the grain sacks off the ground after the combine harvester. The old sack of wheat, in England, weighed $2^{1}/_{4}$cwt, or 252 pounds. It took two good men to lift one off the ground – and a better one to carry it up the granary ladder! Nowadays the heaviest sack allowed in Britain weighs only 100 pounds. The old farm workers would have looked on that as 'boys' work'.*

'Our barns they are full, our fields they are
    clear.
Good health to our master and friends.
We will make no more ado, but we'll plough
    and we'll sow,
And prepare for the very next year!'
                    From A Song for Every Season

ABOVE AND RIGHT: *When all was safely
gathered in! The corn harvest was the
culmination of a year of care and labour, and
it was the custom for the farmer to give a
grand supper for the men and women who
had wrought mightily to plough and to sow, to
reap and to mow.*

LEFT: *The harvest supper was only one of the
many ancient customs connected with the
harvest. Some, such as the making of a corn
dolly (here worn by an unsuspecting
sheepdog) in which the Spirit of the Corn
could dwell until the next harvest, were
unashamedly pagan in origin.*

BELOW: *Back in 1900, when the world was still innocent and young, these charming ladies do not seem to be taking the hay harvest very seriously!*

'We called for a dance and we trippèd it along.
We danced all round the haycocks till the
    rising of the sun.
When the sun did shine such a glorious light
    and the harmless birds did sing,
Each lad he took his lass in hand and went
    back to his haymaking!'